STARS & PLANETS

Dr. Mike Goldsmith

KINGFISHER
NEW YORK

KINGFISHER
LONDON & NEW YORK

Copyright © Kingfisher 2008
Published in the United States by Kingfisher,
175 Fifth Ave., New York, NY 10010
Kingfisher is an imprint of Macmillan Children's Books, London.
All rights reserved.

Illustration by Chris Moore (represented by Artist Partners Ltd.),
Alex Pang, and The Peter Bull Art Studio

First published in 2008 by Kingfisher
First published in paperback in 2011 by Kingfisher

Distributed in the U.S. by Macmillan, 175 Fifth Ave., New York, NY 10010

Library of Congress Cataloging-in-Publication data has been applied for.

ISBN: 978-0-7534-66827

Kingfisher books are available for special promotions and premiums. For details contact:
Special Markets Department, Macmillan, 175 Fifth Ave., New York, NY 10010.

For more information, please visit www.kingfisherbooks.com

Printed in China
10 9 8 7 6 5 4 3 2 1
1TR/0411/WKT/UNTD/140MA

Note to readers: The website addresses listed in this book are correct at the time of publishing.
However, due to the ever-changing nature of the Internet, website addresses and content can change.
Websites can contain links that are unsuitable for children. The publisher cannot be held responsible for
changes in website addresses or content or for information obtained through third-party websites.
We strongly advise that Internet searches are supervised by an adult.

CONTENTS

STAR—a giant ball of gas that generates heat and light

STARS

For thousands of years people have gazed at the starlit sky and asked questions. And for hundreds of years telescopes have shown them the answers—and raised even more questions. When scientists try to understand strange planets and distant stars, they use images that have been sent by telescopes, both those on Earth and those that drift through space high above us.

Observatory

In the desert of Arizona, Kitt Peak National Observatory is the home of 19 optical telescopes. The telescopes use huge mirrors to collect light from stars and form images of them.

Solar panels convert sunlight into electricity to power the Hubble Space Telescope.

Radio telescope

There are many types of light that we cannot see but special telescopes can. This one, in Hawaii, picks up radio waves from the stars. The photograph took several minutes to make. During that time, the stars appeared to circle in the sky as Earth spun on its axis.

Hubble Space Telescope

Many of our best photographs of space have been produced by this optical telescope. The Hubble has been in orbit since 1990, when it traveled into space onboard a space shuttle. It produces much clearer images than Earth-based telescopes are able to. The motion of air in Earth's atmosphere blurs images (this causes stars to appear to twinkle). Floating beyond our atmosphere, the Hubble does not have this problem.

The "forward shell" houses the primary mirror, which collects light and reflects it toward a secondary mirror. This mirror focuses the light onto detectors to create an image.

> The light from most stars takes years to reach us. A star looks as it did long before you were born.

"I observed often, with wondering delight, both the planets and the fixed stars."

Galileo Galilei (1564–1642)
Italian astronomer and physicist

communication antenna to relay information between Hubble and Earth, via satellites in space

http://apod.nasa.gov/apod

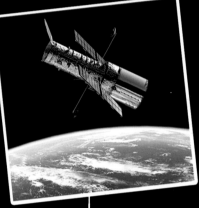

In orbit

The Hubble Space Telescope floats 353 mi. (569km) above our planet. It orbits Earth, which means that it continually follows a path around it. Traveling at 17,360 mph (28,000km/h), it takes 97 minutes to make one orbit.

⬤ THE SUPER-K OBSERVATORY

The universe is full of tiny, fast-moving, invisible objects called neutrinos, which are very difficult to detect. The Super-Kamiokande, or Super-K, Observatory in Japan lies 0.62 mi. (1km) underground and contains 50,000 tons of water. Neutrinos sometimes cause tiny flashes of light in the water. These are detected by the glass tubes that cover the observatory walls.

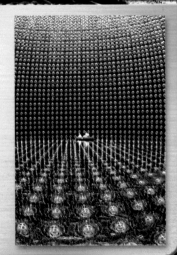

THE UNIVERSE

Around 13.7 billion years ago, the universe began—time, space, and energy appeared, and space expanded rapidly. That expansion, and the fading flash of the beginning of everything, still continues today.

When the universe was cool enough, tiny particles of matter and antimatter formed. By the end of the first second, most of these particles had destroyed each other.

The matter that remained was not spread evenly throughout space. Gradually, the gravity of the denser areas attracted more matter, further increasing their density. Galaxies would later form in these areas, which are shown below in blue.

electrons and positrons created in a laboratory (this happened naturally in the early universe)

The cause of the big bang is science's greatest unsolved mystery.

The universe underwent a sudden jump in the rate of its expansion.

ZERO TIME

LESS THAN ONE TRILLIONTH OF A SECOND

ONE SECOND

100,000 YEARS

Dark matter and dark energy

Most of the universe is invisible because every galaxy is filled with dark matter, which may consist of particles of an unknown type. All of space is filled with dark energy— a mysterious force that opposes the pull of gravity.

The blue glow is dark matter; the pink area is ordinary matter.

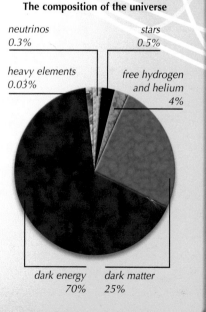

The composition of the universe

neutrinos 0.3%

stars 0.5%

heavy elements 0.03%

free hydrogen and helium 4%

dark energy 70%

dark matter 25%

"The size and age of the cosmos are beyond ordinary human understanding. Lost somewhere between immensity and eternity is our tiny planetary home."

Carl Sagan (1934–1996)
American astronomer and astrochemist

> The Sun is around one third of the age of the universe.

www.bbc.co.uk/science/space/universe/questions_and_ideas/big_bang

When the universe had cooled to around 5,432°F (3,000°C), atoms (mostly hydrogen) formed from smaller particles. Only then could light shine through space.

The first generation of stars formed from hydrogen and helium. During their lives, they built up heavier elements, and when they died—as supernovae—those elements were scattered throughout space. The picture below shows how the formation of the first star may have looked.

The heavy elements from the first stars form part of the Sun and the other stars that exist today. The temperature of the universe today has fallen, after billions of years, to –454°F (–270°C).

380,000 YEARS

300 MILLION YEARS

13.7 BILLION YEARS (TODAY)

The early universe changed very rapidly, and then the pace of change slowed down, so this timeline of key events is not to scale.

⊖ THE BIG CHILL AND THE BIG RIP

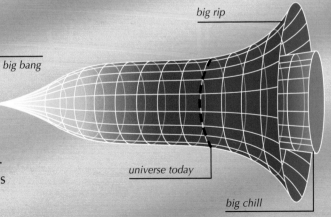

There are two main theories about the future of the universe. It may continue to expand indefinitely, slowing down but never stopping. All the stars would burn out until everything became dark and cold—a big chill. However, there are signs and theories that the rate of the expansion of the universe is increasing. One day, galaxies, stars, planets, and atoms may all tear themselves apart—a big rip.

big rip

big bang

universe today

big chill

GALAXIES

Stars are not spread evenly throughout the
universe—they are grouped into galaxies,
each one containing millions, billions,
or trillions of stars. Many galaxies
are like gigantic whirlpools of
stars, while others are more
like disks, balls, or softly
glowing clouds of light.

GALAXY—a collection of stars, gas, dust, and dark matter

*New stars are
born in the spiral
arms of this galaxy.*

Dwarf galaxy

No one knows for certain
how galaxies form, but it
might be that they begin life
like this young galaxy, which
is much smaller than our
own. The red glow in the
center is the light of ancient
stars, while young new stars
burn blue in the outer regions.

The Whirlpool Galaxy

In spiral galaxies like this, the curving arms,
which are marked by lanes of thick black
dust, are regions of star birth. Like most other
galaxies, the Whirlpool Galaxy is rushing away
from us as the universe expands and the
distances between galaxies grow. Every second,
the galaxy is 310 mi. (500km) farther away.

Andromeda Spiral

This galaxy is the most distant thing that
we can see with the naked eye. It is a
trillion times brighter than the Sun but so
far away (2.5 million light-years) that it
can be seen only on the darkest of nights.

 ❯ Billions of years ago, most galaxies were blue because of the large number of stars forming in them.

This fuzzy glow is a small galaxy passing close to the Whirlpool Galaxy. Its gravity may be triggering star birth in the Whirlpool Galaxy's arms.

Galaxies shine with both visible and invisible radiation. This photograph shows not just visible light but also ultraviolet radiation from new stars in the outer ring and heat radiation from older stars in the core.

⊖ OUR GALAXY—THE MILKY WAY

Our Sun and the solar system lie in one of the Milky Way's outer arms.

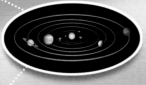

The milky stripe of light in our night sky is our own galaxy, the Milky Way, seen from the inside. The galaxy contains billions of stars, and orbiting some of them are planets that may be similar to those in our own solar system.

From the side, the galaxy would look flat, with the yellow nucleus of older stars bulging in the center.

The Milky Way appears brighter from the Southern Hemisphere, as the South Pole points roughly toward the bright galactic core.

SOLAR SYSTEM

The Sun's web of gravity stretches far out into space, and caught in that web are the planets, moons, rubble, and dust that make up the solar system. Everything in it moves continually around the Sun, with gravity and velocity (motion) in perfect balance.

Building blocks

The inner planets are mostly composed of rock and metal, while the outer planets are mostly made of ice and gas. This is because when the Sun began to shine, the inner regions of the solar system became so hot that only rock and metal worlds could survive there.

MERCURY
(first reached by
Mariner 10 *in 1974)*
Volume: 0.06 Earths
Mass: 0.06 Earths
Day length: 176 Earth days
Year length: 88 Earth days

EARTH
Volume: 1.09×10^{12}km³
Mass: 5.98×10^{24}kg
Day length: 24 hours
Year length: 365.24 days

VENUS
(first reached by
Mariner 2 *in 1962)*
Volume: 0.85 Earths
Mass: 0.82 Earths
Day length: 117 Earth days
Year length: 225 Earth days

MARS
(first reached by
Mariner 4 *in 1965)*
Volume: 0.15 Earths
Mass: 0.11 Earths
Day length: 24 hours 37 mins.
Year length: 687 Earth days

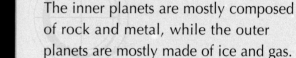

JUPITER
(first reached by
Pioneer 10 *in 1973)*
Volume: 1,266 Earths
Mass: 318 Earths
Day length: 9 hours 55 mins.
Year length: 12 Earth years

Distances from the Sun

The planets closer to the Sun are also closer to each other. The solar system began life as a cloud of dust and gas, and the Sun formed in its densest area. So the region that is closest to our star had more materials with which to build planets.

Earth
93 million mi.
(150 million km)

Venus
67 million mi.
(108 million km)

Mars
141 million mi.
(228 million km)

Jupiter
482 million mi.
(778 million km)

SUN

Mercury
36 million mi.
(58 million km)

Saturn
855 million mi.
(1.43 billion km)

> Billions of years ago, there were dozens of planets in the solar system.

⊖ THE VIEW FROM OUTER SPACE

If we were able to step outside the solar system and look at it as a whole, the sunlit realm of the planets would be too tiny to see. Beyond the planets lies the ring-shaped Kuiper Belt, which is made up of icy objects. The Kuiper Belt merges into the Oort cloud—an enormous area shaped like a hollow sphere that contains the cores of comets. The entire solar system is around two light-years across.

empty region

cross section of
the Oort cloud, which
surrounds the solar system

"We have swept through
all of the planets in the solar
system, from Mercury to Neptune,
in a historic 20 [to] 30 year age
of spacecraft discovery."

Carl Sagan (1934–1996)
American astronomer and astrochemist

SATURN
(first reached by
Pioneer 11 *in 1979)*

Volume: 752 Earths
Mass: 95 Earths
Day length: 10 hours 39 mins.
Year length: 29.5 Earth years

NEPTUNE
(first reached by
Voyager 2 *in 1989)*

Volume: 59 Earths
Mass: 17 Earths
Day length: 16 hours 7 mins.
Year length: 165 Earth years

URANUS
(first reached by
Voyager 2 *in 1986)*

Volume: 64 Earths
Mass: 15 Earths
Day length: 17 hours 14 mins.
Year length: 84 Earth years

Uranus
1.78 billion mi.
(2.87 billion km)

Neptune
2.79 billion mi.
(4.5 billion km)

THE SUN

The Sun is a huge ball of glowing gas, so large that one million Earths would fit inside it. Without its light and heat, there would be no life on Earth and even our atmosphere would lie frozen solid on the ground. Although it is 93 million mi. (150 million km) away, its light is still bright enough to damage our eyes. As the world spins around each day, the Sun moves across our skies.

SUN—our star, around which Earth and the other planets of our solar system orbit

Nuclear furnace

The Sun is mostly made of a light substance called hydrogen. Deep in its core, reactions like those in nuclear bombs convert the hydrogen into helium and release the enormous energy that we see as sunlight.

Light shows

The Sun sends out tiny particles, as well as light and heat. Close to the North and South poles of Earth, these particles are caught in our planet's magnetic field, producing strange, colored lights in the night sky. These spectacular displays are called auroras.

Every second, the Sun becomes four million tons lighter.

Sun sailing

The Sun's light gently presses against everything that it touches. Solar sails are light and shiny craft that drift through space, pushed by sunlight as sailboats are pushed by the wind.

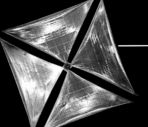

Solar prominence

A prominence is a gigantic cloud of glowing gas—much larger than Earth—that floats in the Sun's atmosphere.

Sunspots are dark patches caused by the Sun's powerful magnetic field. They are darker than the rest of the Sun because they are cooler.

> "One result of the evolution of our Sun . . . will very likely be the reduction of our Earth to a bleak, charred cinder."
>
> **Carl Sagan (1934–1996)**
> ***American astronomer and astrochemist***

The temperature of the Sun's surface is around 9,932°F (5,500°C).

Solar eclipse

Every few months, the Moon passes directly between the Sun and Earth. When this happens, the Sun appears to turn black and the glow of its corona appears around it (see right). At other times, the corona is too dim to see against the Sun's bright light.

MERCURY AND VENUS

YEAR—the time that it takes for a planet to orbit the Sun once

Mercury and Venus are much closer to the Sun than we are, which means that they are much hotter than Earth. They also move more quickly around the Sun than we do, so their years are shorter than ours.

Colorful craters?

Like many photographs taken in space, this *Mariner 10* image has been falsely colored to show the different features more clearly.

metal-rich area

solidified lava flow

Kuiper crater

No data has been recorded for this area, so it is left blank in images of the planet.

Mercury

Mercury, the smallest planet and the closest to the Sun, cools rapidly at night because it has almost no atmosphere. So, while the temperature can reach 806°F (430°C) by day, nights are even colder than Antarctica. This image pieces together photographs taken by the *Mariner 10* probe, which traveled to Mercury in 1974. It discovered that the planet is rocky and heavily cratered.

The surface of Mercury is marked with wrinkles. These probably formed when the planet cooled and shrunk soon after it formed.

> Although Mercury is much closer to the Sun than Venus, Venus is actually the hotter planet.

Mapping Venus

The thick clouds of Venus always hide the surface of the planet from our telescopes. So, in 1989, the *Magellan* probe was sent to orbit the planet and map it by radar. It revealed that all of Venus's surface is young— only half a billion years old.

Lava domes

Many of the features that *Magellan* discovered on Venus are caused by volcanic activity. These domes are like nothing known on any other planet. They may have been caused by lava welling up under the ground, causing the surface to stretch and rise.

The *Magellan* probe orbited Venus for four years.

Only flashes of lightning brighten Venus's dark and cloudy surface.

www.space.com/mercury and www.windows2universe.org/venus/venus.html

The 3-D maps of Venus produced by the Magellan probe show that most of its rocky surface is made up of smooth volcanic plains.

Maat Mons, the highest volcano on Venus

Venus

Venus, our closest neighbor, was once thought to be similar to Earth in prehistoric times. In fact, Venus is a deadly planet with an atmosphere that is as dense as our oceans. Rain of sulfuric acid falls from the cloudy, yellow sky, boiling away before even reaching the ground. The greenhouse effect heats the planet's surface to 896°F (480°C).

EARTH

The distance of Earth from the Sun is what makes life on our planet possible. Living things need liquid water, and if we were much farther from the Sun, all our water would be frozen like it is on Mars. If we were a little closer, water would boil as it would on Venus.

As the world is gradually heating up, our polar ice is melting. This causes flooding in low-lying areas.

Plants and trees produce oxygen, which all animals need in order to breathe. Plants also absorb the waste gases that animals breathe out.

LIQUID—a state of matter in which a substance is runny, taking the shape of its container and forming a surface inside it

Earth's atmosphere

An atmosphere is the layer of gases that is held around a planet by the force of its gravity. Earth's atmospheric gases keep the surface warm at night and protect it from dangerous Sun rays during the day. The atmosphere also helps move water around. When water evaporates from the oceans, clouds form in the lowest layer of the atmosphere. The clouds bring rain to the land.

"We do not inherit the Earth from our ancestors; we borrow it from our children."

Haida Indian saying

> If all the ice on Earth melted, the oceans would rise by 328 ft. (100m).

Life has existed on Earth for more than three billion years. People evolved only around 200,000 years ago, but they have transformed the entire planet. At night, the glow from city lights can be seen from space.

THE SEASONS

Because Earth tilts on its axis, while one hemisphere is angled toward the Sun, the other hemisphere is angled away from it. So, when one hemisphere experiences summer, the other hemisphere has winter. These seasons change as Earth completes its yearly orbit of the Sun. Night and day are caused by Earth spinning on its axis—it takes 24 hours for the planet to complete one rotation.

The Northern Hemisphere, angled away from the Sun, experiences winter.

axis

equator

day **night**

The Southern Hemisphere, angled toward the Sun, experiences summer.

Shifting plates

Deep beneath your feet, Earth is so hot that the rock is liquid. On this fiery sea, huge areas of stone, called plates, float. As the plates slowly crunch into each other, they cause volcanoes and earthquakes.

There are more than two million species of life on Earth, each one adapted to live in a particular place, like these penguins in their frozen home.

MARS

Mars, the "red planet," has fascinated people for more than 100 years, ever since astronomers thought that they saw canals there, built by an alien civilization. The canals were an illusion, but our fascination with the possibility of life on Mars has remained. Mars is the second-closest planet to us (Venus is our nearest neighbor), and it is the planet that is the most like our own, with icecaps, seasons, volcanoes, and deserts. Once, long ago, it had lakes and rivers, too—and possibly even Martians!

A mast supports the panoramic camera system, which will help the rover navigate an area of several miles.

solar panel

In 1976, a probe, *Viking 2*, landed on Mars and took this photograph, which shows a pink sky, caused by the red dust particles in the air.

The six wheels are rugged in order to cope with the planet's rocky terrain.

ExoMars

The *ExoMars* rover is due to begin its exploration of the red planet in 2016 as part of a European Space Agency (ESA) project. The rover will be delivered by an orbiter and will use either balloons or parachutes to slow down its descent so that it lands safely. The rover will continue the studies of the planet's rocks, building on *Viking 2*'s discovery that Martian soil is full of chemicals that would burn human skin.

Mars is red because it is rusty. Long ago, iron in its desert soil combined with oxygen and painted the entire planet red.

☉ICE ON MARS

This bright blue patch is a frozen pool of ice. It lies in a crater in Mars's vast northern plains. The photograph was taken by ESA's *Mars Express Orbiter* in 2005. Water cannot exist in liquid form because the planet's atmospheric pressure is currently too low.

This artist's impression of the orbiter shows the antenna used to communicate with Earth.

This instrument uses radar waves to "see" up to 0.6 mi (1km) beneath the planet's surface.

solar panel to power orbiter

Mars *Reconnaissance Orbiter*

Many spacecraft from Earth have visited Mars—this is the *Reconnaissance Orbiter*. It arrived in 2006, and it still circles the planet today. Its mission is to take pictures of the surface of Mars, monitor the weather, and study the rocks and ice. It is also looking for the best places for future spacecraft to land. One day, it will be used to pass messages from other missions back to Earth.

The frozen north

The *Reconnaissance Orbiter* took this photograph of Mars's northern polar region. It shows steep cliffs, more than 1 mi. (2km) high, cloaked in ice.

Mars has permanently frozen ice at both its south and north poles. Like on Earth, the icecaps grow or shrink according to the season.

"If [Mars rovers] find a rock that proves there was once life on Mars, it will be, without any doubt, the greatest scientific discovery ever made."

David McNab and James Younger
writers and science-documentary producers

Jupiter's Great Red Spot is a giant hurricane—much larger than Earth—that has raged for hundreds of years.

Ganymede, the largest moon in the solar system, is bigger than Mercury.

Callisto is mostly made of ice.

Io is sprinkled with erupting volcanoes.

Europa has liquid seas under its icy crust.

JUPITER AND SATURN

Jupiter and Saturn are gas giants—huge worlds with deep atmospheres concealing cores of rock and ice. Both have rings—Jupiter's rings are faint dust belts, whereas Saturn's rings are made of rocky ice—and both have at least 60 moons each. The planets spin so fast that they have very short days and the flattened-sphere shape of a grapefruit. Both are still cooling from their formation, and this leftover heat generates storms that never end.

Many moons

Jupiter has at least 63 moons, and many of them are locked by gravity so that one side always faces the planet. Some, such as Io, are warmed by the stretching and squeezing effects of Jupiter's gravity. Others crumble into space, their dust forming rings around the planet.

∨ CORE—*the central part of a planet*

> Jupiter is large enough to contain all the other planets.

Jupiter

Jupiter is the giant planet of our solar system, more massive than all of the others combined. Although it is more than four times as far from us as the Sun, it can be the brightest object in the night sky. Jupiter is surrounded by a zone of deadly radiation and an enormous magnetic field.

Light world

Although Saturn weighs more than 95 times the weight of Earth, it is still the lightest planet for its size in the solar system. It is so light that it would float in water.

Saturn's rings are shown in false color here. The pink rings contain only large rocks; the green and blue rings include smaller fragments as well.

Saturn

Saturn's ring system is composed of billions of orbiting fragments of icy rock that range in size from dust particles to boulders. They may be the remains of a moon-size object that strayed too close to Saturn and was torn apart by the planet's gravity.

URANUS AND NEPTUNE

The two outermost planets in our solar system, Uranus and Neptune, are gas giants like Jupiter and Saturn. Far out in space the Sun shines dimly, so these worlds are cold and dark. As they move slowly around the Sun in huge orbits, they have long years—Uranus's year is 84 Earth years long and Neptune's is 165.

ORBIT—the path of one object around another object in space

Uranus

Uranus was discovered in 1781 by English astronomer William Herschel (1738–1822) and reached by a space probe 197 years later. This giant planet, circled by dark rings of black boulders, gets its green color from the methane in its atmosphere. Uranus spins on its back, probably knocked over by a collision with a wandering planet billions of years ago.

Miranda, a moon of Uranus

Miranda's surface is so jumbled that some scientists think the moon was shattered long ago and then reassembled when gravity pulled the fragments together again.

On some parts of Uranus, night can last for more than 40 Earth years.

Voyages to remote worlds

The twin Voyager space probes, *Voyager 1* and *Voyager 2*, explored the outer planets in the 1970s and 1980s. Both probes will travel beyond the solar system for many thousands of years—although they will cease to function in the 2020s. In around 40,000 years, *Voyager 2* will reach a nearby star.

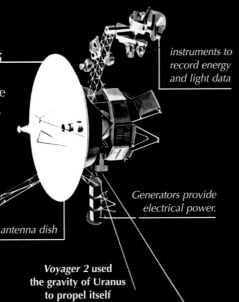

instruments to record energy and light data

Generators provide electrical power.

antenna dish

A magnetometer on the arm measures magnetic forces.

***Voyager 2* used the gravity of Uranus to propel itself toward Neptune.**

"I saw, O, first of all mankind,
I saw the disk of my new planet gliding there
beyond our tumults, in that realm of peace."

Herschel's discovery of Uranus
from Alfred Noyes's poem The Torch Bearers, 1937

Huge white clouds of methane ice rush across a dark storm system on the face of Neptune, the windiest planet in the solar system.

www.space.com/uranus and www.space.com/neptune

Neptune

The color of the outermost planet in our solar system gives it its name—Neptune, god of the blue sea. Unlike the other giants, some of Neptune's rings are incomplete arcs. This cold planet generates some heat of its own, and this powers its dramatic weather systems. However, its largest moon, Triton, may be the coldest moon in the solar system.

Nitrogen, which makes up most of our air, is mostly frozen solid on Neptune's moon Triton. However, sometimes it squirts upward as liquid jets, before being knocked sideways by high-altitude winds.

SPACE RUBBLE

The solar system contains one star, eight planets, around 170 moons—and billions of other objects, ranging from tiny grains of dust to lumps of ice, rock, or metal hundreds of miles wide. This rubble is the solar system's leftover building material, and most of it has remained unchanged for billions of years. It is made up of dwarf planets, comets, meteoroids, asteroids, and Kuiper Belt objects.

As comets (lumps of grit and ice) get close to the Sun, their surfaces boil and crumble, releasing dusts and gases that form tails. The faint blue tail behind comet Hale-Bopp is gas; the brighter tail is dust.

Shooting stars (meteors) are the trails of small pieces of falling space rubble (meteoroids) that glow as they burn up in our atmosphere.

This far above Earth, there is no atmosphere in which the asteroid can burn up. The fiery trail has been caused by nuclear missiles sent from Earth in an attempt to destroy the asteroid.

Mimas, a moon of Saturn, was almost destroyed by the object that crashed into it and created this enormous crater.

● DWARF PLANET PLUTO

Pluto and the largest of its three moons, Charon (on right)

Pluto, discovered in 1930, is one of the solar system's three known dwarf planets, which are small, round worlds. Its oval orbit means that its distance from the Sun varies greatly, and at times Pluto is closer to the Sun than Neptune. When it is a long way out in space, Pluto becomes so cold that its atmosphere freezes solid.

> Comet Hyakutake had a tail more than 353 million mi. (570 million km) long—four times the distance between Earth and the Sun.

The destruction of Earth

Throughout its history, Earth has been the target of many asteroids. The impact of one is believed to have caused the extinction of the dinosaurs, and another of a similar size could mean the end of human civilization. Scientists are tracking the orbits of asteroids—if one ever appears to be on a collision course with our planet, it might be disintegrated by nuclear weapons or pushed or pulled off course with rockets or solar sails (see page 13).

Barringer Crater

This crater, in Arizona, was formed by the impact of a meteorite around 50,000 years ago. It is around 4,000 ft. (1,200m) wide.

"Our missiles have failed. The comets are still headed for Earth, and there's nothing we can do to stop them . . . The impact is going to be . . . well, disastrous."

From the 1998 movie *Deep Impact*

www.bbc.co.uk/science/space/solarsystem/other_solar_system_bodies/asteroid

SPACE CLOUDS

When people started to study the night sky with telescopes, they found fuzzy patches that they called nebulae, meaning "clouds." Many of these nebulae really are clouds— of glowing or dark dust or gas. They are places of star birth or star death. Other nebulae are nearby clusters of stars, and some are distant galaxies.

Pillars of Creation

In these giant columns of dust and gas, which form part of the Eagle Nebula, new stars are being born. Powerful radiation from hot young stars nearby heats the outer layers of the columns to form the bluish-green mist that can be seen around them.

Star birth

This telescope image shows a wider view of the Eagle Nebula with an exploding star at its glowing core. Exploding stars (supernovae) squeeze parts of surrounding cloud, creating dense regions. Gravity continues the process, and the squeezed regions get more and more dense. They also get hotter—their centers get so hot that nuclear reactions begin, turning these central areas into stars.

Small protusions contain globules of dense gas that are the beginnings of new stars.

Many of the atoms that we are made of spent millions of years in a molecular cloud after forming in an exploding star.

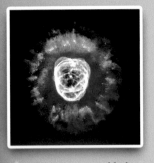

At only 1,000 years old, the Eskimo Nebula is very young. Astronomer William Herschel discovered it in 1787. Later, he described spherical nebulae like the Eskimo as "planetary nebulae."

A planetary nebula, which is gas thrown off by a star, is usually sphere shaped. The Cat's Eye Nebula, however, has a much more complex shape. No one is sure why.

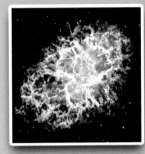

The Crab Nebula is the remains of a supernova— a massive star exploding at the end of its life. The light from the explosion reached Earth in 1054.

The Orion Nebula is the easiest to see from Earth. This detail shows the Horsehead, a dark cloud of dust silhouetted against the glow of a hot gas cloud called an emission nebula.

Each pillar is around one light-year long. This means that it would take light one year to travel from the top to the bottom.

". . . the nebulae [are] amazing us by the strangeness of their forms and the incomprehensibility of their nature . . ."

Mary Somerville (1780–1872)
Scottish science writer

The Pillars may no longer exist—a nearby supernova explosion might have destroyed them 6,000 years ago. If so, we will not see that destruction for 1,000 years, since the Pillars are 7,000 light-years away.

http://hubblesite.org/gallery/album/nebula

⊖ BRIGHT DUST SHELLS

Many aging stars throw off shells of dust, and many others flash and pulse with light. These images show both: the central star has sent a burst of light that is spreading gradually through the dust shells, lighting up one after another.

The red glow in the center of the dust shells is a supergiant star.

The black regions are holes in the dust shells.

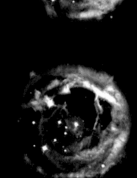

The outermost dust shell is around the size of Jupiter.

Blue giant

A blue giant, 1,000 times larger than the Sun, is as hot as a star can be without destroying itself. Its incredible power boils away its atmosphere and floods the region around it with harsh blue light and deadly radiation.

STRANGE STARS

The Sun is a very ordinary star that has changed little in temperature or brightness during the history of life on Earth. This is lucky for us—if it had changed much, we would probably not be here to see it. But many other stars are strange—they pulsate, change shape, connect together, or blow apart. And while some are incredibly hot, others barely smolder.

PULSATE—to grow regularly larger and smaller

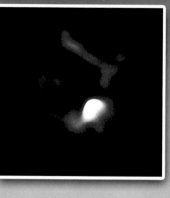

Carbon star

Some cool, red stars have atmospheres that are rich in carbon, which condenses around them in the form of sooty clouds. The clouds filter the light of their parent star, making its glow an even deeper red.

Distorted star

Not all stars are round. Mira (from the Latin for "wonderful") looks distorted. This is either because it changes shape as it pulsates or because some of its surface is too dark to see.

 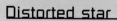 The largest known star, VY Canis Majoris, is big enough to hold around ten billion Suns.

Contact binaries

Binary stars—a pair of stars that orbit each other—are very common. However, it is rare to find any that are so close that they touch, like these pictured here. Stars that do touch each other share each other's atmospheres and distort each other's shapes.

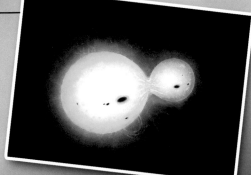

Variables and demons

When stars change in brightness, they are called variables. Some variable stars suddenly flash with light or are darkened by clouds of dust. Other stars brighten and dim regularly. This may be caused by other, dimmer stars orbiting them and blocking their light. The first such star to be discovered is called Algol, from the Arabic word for "demon."

The brown dwarf is bound by gravity to this bigger and brighter red dwarf.

Brown dwarf

Brown dwarfs are dim objects, heavier than planets but lighter than true stars. Strangely, although their masses range from 20 to 80 times that of Jupiter, they are all around the same size.

> "Classifying the stars has helped materially in all studies of the structure of the universe . . ."

Annie Jump Cannon (1863–1941)
American astronomer

⊖ PULSATING STARS

Astronomers can figure out the average true brightnesses of Cepheid stars, which appear to pulsate, from the time that they take to fade and brighten. Taking into account the fact that all stars look dimmer the farther away they are, the scientists can then figure out the stars' distances from Earth.

A pulsating star is hottest and brightest when it is small.

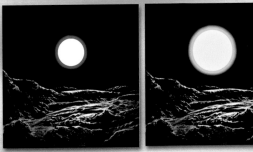

As the star swells, it fades, cools, and reddens.

Some stars take only a few hours to swell and shrink; others take several years.

DEATH

Stars are like factories, converting hydrogen to helium, helium to other elements, and producing floods of energy to light up our skies by day and night. This nuclear processing may continue steadily for billions of years. However, eventually, further conversion of elements becomes impossible, and stars die. But they don't go quietly . . .

When there is no fuel left to burn, the outer layers of a red giant swell, forming a bubblelike "planetary nebula" (which actually has nothing to do with planets).

The nebula is made of such thin gas that its core—a white dwarf—can be seen. The white dwarf, which will take billions of years to cool, is the final stage in the life of medium- and small-size stars.

The Hourglass Nebula was probably shaped by wind expansion in a cloud that was denser at its poles than at its equator.

When the hydrogen fuel in the core of stars with a similar mass to the Sun runs out, nuclear reactions in outer layers take over. This causes the star to swell and cool, turning it into a red giant.

Stars burn for millions or billions of years—the more massive they are, the quicker they burn up and the shorter their lives are.

Two paths to death

What happens when a star dies depends on its mass. Stars like the Sun swell enormously, melting and engulfing their closest planets (see path from left to above). More massive stars die in supernova explosions that are brighter than galaxies (see path from left to right). Supernovae can both trigger the birth of new stars and provide the building materials for them.

When they run out of hydrogen, massive stars swell up into supergiants—perhaps one million times the volume of the Sun and 100,000 times brighter. Many supergiants are pulsating variables, brightening as they shrink and fading as they swell.

The first pulsar was labeled LGM-1—"Little Green Men"—as some people thought that its signal was an alien message.

"And all about the cosmic sky,
The black that lies beyond our blue,
Dead stars innumerable lie,
And stars of red and angry hue,
Not dead but doomed to die."

Julian Huxley (1887–1975)
English biologist and poet

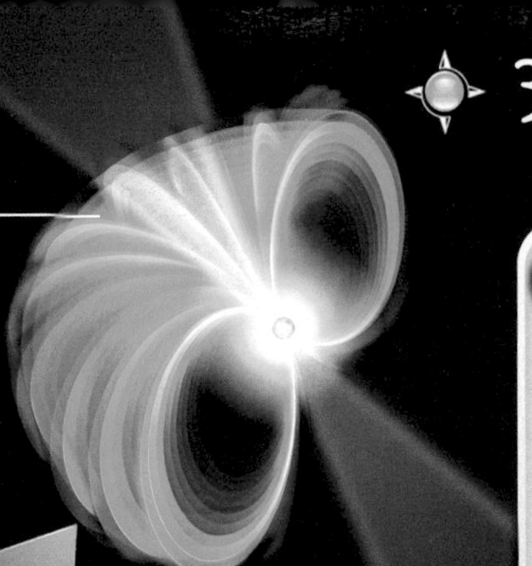

Neutron stars are dead stars that form from the remains of supernovae. They are heavier than white dwarfs but lighter than black holes. A pulsar is a neutron star with a magnetic field that funnels radio waves into beams.

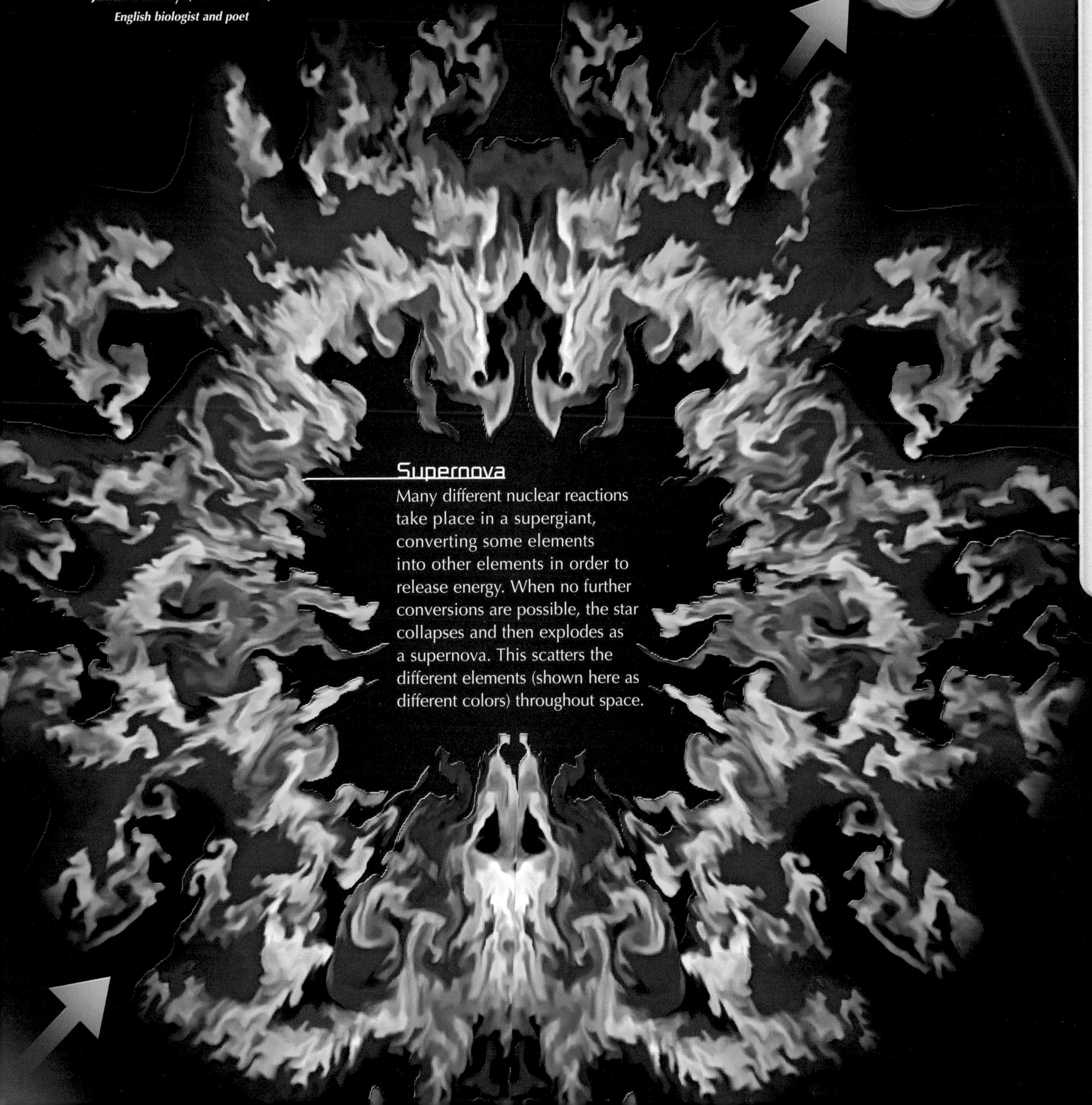

Supernova

Many different nuclear reactions take place in a supergiant, converting some elements into other elements in order to release energy. When no further conversions are possible, the star collapses and then explodes as a supernova. This scatters the different elements (shown here as different colors) throughout space.

http://burro.astr.cwru.edu/stu/stars_lifedeath.html

Not all black holes
are deadly. If a black hole
spins fast enough, a spacecraft
on the correct route could take
a shortcut to another part of the
universe—or even to another time.

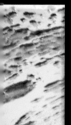

SPACE WARPS

One hundred years ago, Albert Einstein showed that space and time are locked together into "space-time" and that space-time is warped around massive objects. These warps are what we usually call gravity. The smooth warps made by the Sun guide the planets in their orbits—but not all space warps are so gentle . . .

Space-time

Imagine space-time as a stretched rubber sheet. Stars and planets warp the sheet as they sink into it. A fast object passing through a dip in space-time will change direction, while a slower one will roll around the inside of the dip in orbit. An even slower object will spiral down into the dip.

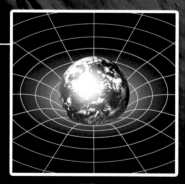

Wormholes

The more mass there is, the more warped space-time becomes. If enough mass is concentrated into a small area, it can push through the folds of space-time like a needle. This creates a connection between one place and time in the universe and another—a wormhole.

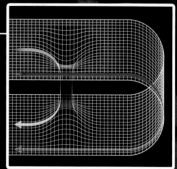

> The universe is full of wormholes that are too tiny to see.

http://hubblesite.org/explore_astronomy/black_holes

The gravity close to a black hole changes greatly over short distances, distorting nearby objects into long, thin shapes before dragging them in. This is called spaghettification.

Black hole

In a normal star, the inward pull of gravity is balanced by the outward pressure of radiation. But when the star's fuel is exhausted and the radiation fades, gravity can no longer be resisted, and the star collapses inward. This causes the star's density to grow, and as it grows, the pull of its gravity increases. Eventually, in the most massive stars, all nearby objects are dragged into the star. Even light cannot escape the pull, so the star becomes black—a black hole.

SPACE PIONEERS

After the U.S.S.R. surprised the world by reaching space first, the U.S.A. competed with them to send machines, animals, and finally humans into orbit and onto the Moon. Space travel has many practical benefits, but it is also the urge to explore the unknown universe that drives people onward—and outward—to other worlds.

escape rocket (for use in a launch emergency)

Apollo 11's command module (under a protective covering)

service module

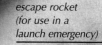

Sputnik

On October 4, 1957, satellite *Sputnik 1*, a 185-lb. (84-kg) sphere, was blasted into space from the U.S.S.R. The first artificial object to orbit Earth, the beep of its radio transmitter could be picked up all over the planet. The Space Age had begun.

antenna for transmitting radio signals to Earth

Every nine seconds, the *Saturn V* rocket burned enough fuel to fill a swimming pool.

The lunar module, Eagle, is inside this section.

Apollo 11: mission to the Moon

The lunar landing in 1969 was possibly the most important event in history—the Moon is the first new world we have reached. The enormous *Saturn V* rocket launched the *Apollo 11* spaceship and its three-man crew across more than 186,000 mi. (300,000km) of space. One after another, the three sections of the *Saturn V* ran out of fuel and were left behind, leaving the three Apollo modules to continue their voyage to the Moon.

The fastest that humans have ever traveled is 6.7 mi. per second (10.8km/s)—the speed that the crew of *Apollo 8* achieved in 1968.

U.S.S.R. the Union of Soviet Socialist Republics, or the Soviet Union (1922–1991). Russia was its largest member.

> "That's one small step for a man; one giant leap for mankind."

Neil Armstrong (born 1930)
Commander of Apollo 11, July 20, 1969

Yuri Gagarin, a 27-year-old Russian pilot, became the first human in space in 1961. His *Vostok 1* spaceship, called *Swallow*, took him around Earth and returned him most of the way home: he parachuted the last few miles, landing in a farmer's field.

Gagarin waits to be launched into space.

service module

command module

Journey's end

After a three-day journey, *Apollo 11*'s command-and-service module (CSM) reached the Moon and went into orbit around it. Astronauts Neil Armstrong and Buzz Aldrin moved into the lunar module, *Eagle*, and piloted it down to the surface, leaving Michael Collins onboard the CSM.

Apollo 17's CSM (above) was similar to Apollo 11's.

The *Eagle* has landed

The astronauts guided the lunar module, *Eagle*, to a safe landing on the Moon's Sea of Tranquillity.

thruster (one of four)

fuel tank

Only this top section of the Eagle returned to the CSM. The rest is still on the Moon.

foil to reflect sunlight and stop the Eagle from overheating

landing pad

Aldrin, standing on the Moon, checks equipment on the Eagle.

BEYOND THE SKY

The rockets that took men to the Moon were enormous—and enormously expensive. And they could be used only once. For regular trips to the region of space close to Earth, whether to repair satellites or to visit space stations, craft that can be reused are needed. Spaceships like these may one day allow anyone to be an astronaut.

SATELLITE—an orbiting object, either artificial or natural like the Moon

Shuttles have large launch bays for transporting satellites and equipment, which are lifted into orbit by a robotic arm.

USA

NASA
Atlantis

The external tank contains liquid fuel. After use, it is released and burns up in the atmosphere.

> In space, the shuttle's robotic arm can move satellites more massive than trucks, but on Earth, it cannot even lift up itself.

The space shuttle

The space shuttle, created by the U.S. space agency NASA, is a reusable spaceship that can orbit Earth. It has been used for launching, retrieving, and repairing satellites, traveling to space stations, and for research. It takes off like a rocket but lands back on Earth like an airplane. The 30-year-old shuttle program was due to end in 2010, but the shuttle will continue to be used in the construction of the International Space Station at least until the end of 2011.

Shuttle astronauts use nitrogen thrusters to move around freely in space.

www.nasa.gov/mission_pages/shuttle/vehicle/index.html

When their solid fuel has burned up, the two rocket boosters fall to Earth by parachute. They are refilled and reused.

SpaceShipOne

SpaceShipOne is an experimental space plane launched in 2004. It reached a height of more than 60 mi. (100km) and flew more than three times faster than the speed of sound. A larger, more powerful version called *SpaceShipTwo* is now the basis of a commercial space-flight program due to begin in late 2011.

The tail folds upward on reentry into Earth's atmosphere to reduce speed.

New horizons

The *Orion* spaceship is being developed to travel not only to the International Space Station (ISS) but to the Moon and Mars, too. Like the shuttle, it is a reusable craft.

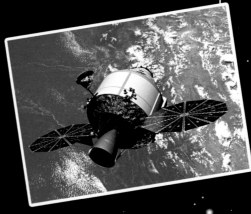

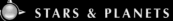

CITIES IN THE SKY

People are living high up above your head right now in the International Space Station (ISS)—the latest in a series of space stations that began in 1971 with the Soviet *Salyut 1*. The Americans followed with *Skylab*, an orbiting laboratory, in 1973. Today space stations are mostly used for space research, but in the future they will be hotels—and the first steppingstone for long-distance space explorers.

"Earth is the cradle of humanity, but one cannot live in the cradle forever."

Konstantin Tsiolkovsky (1857–1935)
Russian rocket scientist

Onboard the ISS

The ISS is being constructed in orbit by 16 countries. Onboard, the astronauts and other objects are almost weightless, and the effects of this "microgravity" on people, plants, crystals, fluids, and flames will be studied, helping plan future space colonies. Day-to-day life in the ISS is a constant experiment in weightlessness. Without the resistance of gravity, astronauts must exercise to stop their bones and muscles from weakening. In 2007, astronaut Sunita Williams ran a marathon on the ISS's treadmill.

Spinning through space

The International Space Station orbits Earth, but in the future stations could use the energy of the Sun to power themselves on long missions to other worlds. Generations of explorers could live their entire lives onboard, harnessing the Sun's light and warmth to grow food. A spinning craft like this one would generate its own gravity for its inhabitants.

> The longest space flight—by Russian cosmonaut Valeriy Polyakov on the space station *Mir*—was 437 days long.

⊖ BUILDING A SPACE STATION

The ISS is continually being assembled from separate modules, which are blasted into space on shuttles. The first module went into orbit in 1998, and the station has been permanently crewed since the first astronauts arrived in 2000. When it is finished, the ISS will be the size of a soccer field. The station is powered by solar panels, which convert sunlight into electricity.

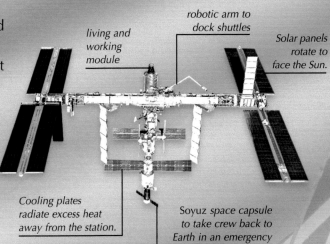

living and working module

robotic arm to dock shuttles

Solar panels rotate to face the Sun.

Cooling plates radiate excess heat away from the station.

Soyuz space capsule to take crew back to Earth in an emergency

www.nasa.gov/externalFlash/ISSRG

Astronauts construct the ISS, 211 mi. (340km) above New Zealand.

STARSHIPS

Traveling to the stars is easy—in fact, the *Pioneer* and *Voyager* unmanned planetary probes are on their way now, heading for the farthest reaches of the solar system and interstellar space beyond. So, crossing great distances is not the problem. The challenge is not space, but time—the probes will travel for tens of thousands of years before reaching a star. So, in order for people to explore other star systems, faster ships are needed.

Mining in space

The raw materials needed to make and fuel starships could one day be mined from asteroids—some of which are made entirely of metal. Their low gravity would make the materials almost weightless, so they would be **easy to remove. Here, four robot craft are moving an asteroid past Mars on its way to Earth.**

Landing craft

Starships will not be designed to land on other worlds. Instead, crews will descend to planets in short-range shuttle craft that have streamlined shapes for flying through planetary atmospheres.

> The closest star is around one million times farther from Earth than the closest planet.

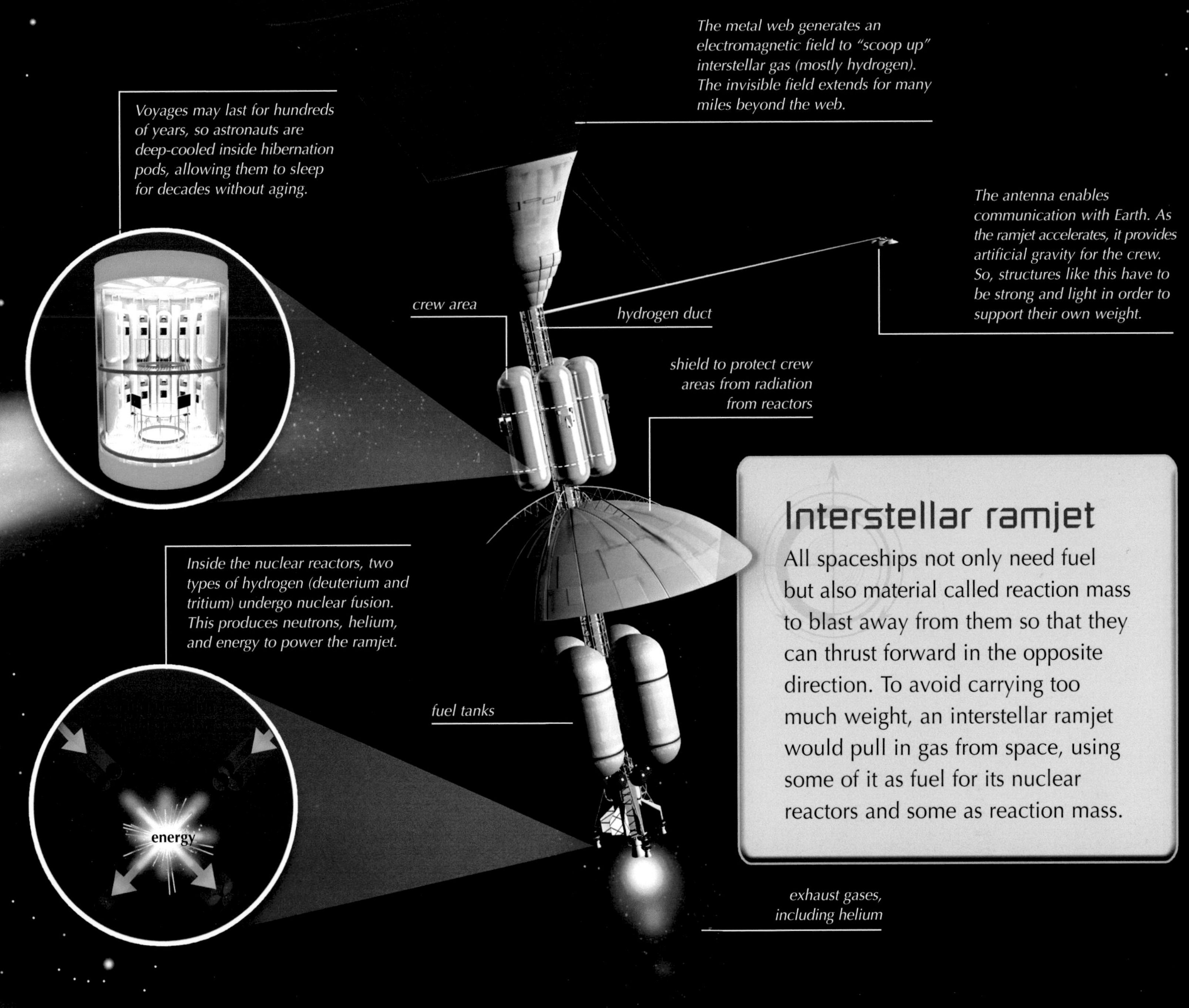

The metal web generates an electromagnetic field to "scoop up" interstellar gas (mostly hydrogen). The invisible field extends for many miles beyond the web.
Voyages may last for hundreds of years, so astronauts are deep-cooled inside hibernation pods, allowing them to sleep for decades without aging.
The antenna enables communication with Earth. As the ramjet accelerates, it provides artificial gravity for the crew. So, structures like this have to be strong and light in order to support their own weight.
crew area
hydrogen duct
shield to protect crew areas from radiation from reactors
Inside the nuclear reactors, two types of hydrogen (deuterium and tritium) undergo nuclear fusion. This produces neutrons, helium, and energy to power the ramjet.
energy
fuel tanks
exhaust gases, including helium

Interstellar ramjet

All spaceships not only need fuel but also material called reaction mass to blast away from them so that they can thrust forward in the opposite direction. To avoid carrying too much weight, an interstellar ramjet would pull in gas from space, using some of it as fuel for its nuclear reactors and some as reaction mass.

www.nasa.gov/centers/glenn/technology/warp/warp.html

LIFE BEYOND

Is Earth the only place where life exists? In search of an answer, robots sift through the sands of Mars, signals are beamed to distant stars, probes carry messages on disks and plaques, and powerful radio telescopes scan the skies.

PROBE—an uncrewed spaceship sent to explore other worlds

Wormlike animals prey on the microscopic creatures that cluster around volcanic vents. The vents provide the warmth that living things need.

Free-swimming organisms use light in order to communicate.

> Germlike structures have been found in a Martian meteorite.

Life on a distant moon?

The moon Europa is warmed by the gravity of Jupiter, the planet that it orbits. This means that under its icy surface a huge ocean lies hidden. In its warm darkness it is just possible that life exists. On Earth, too, there are creatures in the deep ocean that obtain their energy from underground heat.

The transporter has drilled and melted its way through Europa's icy surface.

The robot probe has sensors, thrusters, and grippers.

⊖ POSTCARDS TO ALIENS

The space probes *Pioneer 10* and *Pioneer 11*, which were launched in 1972 and 1973 respectively, each carry a steel plate with picture messages for any creatures that might find them.

humans, in front of diagram of probe to show scale

star map showing Sun's position in galaxy

solar system

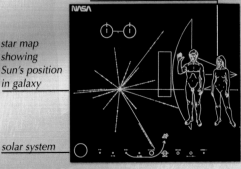

image on a plaque onboard the *Pioneer 10* probe

SIGNALS TO THE STARS ⊖

Earth's population in 1974: 4.2 billion

human

average height of human: 5 ft. 10 in. (1,764mm)

Sun and planets of our solar system

Arecibo telescope

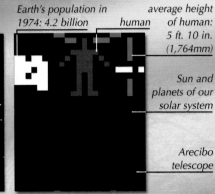

part of the binary-coded Arecibo message

In 1974, the Arecibo radio telescope sent this message to a large group of stars. It will arrive there around A.D. 27,000. (Color has been added here to show the different pictures.)

GLOSSARY

antenna
A radio antenna is a device that sends or receives radio signals.

asteroid
A small rocky or metallic world orbiting the Sun. Asteroids are mostly found between the orbits of Mars and Jupiter.

atmosphere
Layer of gases around a star, planet, or moon.

atom
The smallest part of an element, composed of a nucleus made of protons and neutrons. Electrons are arranged around the nucleus.

axis
An imaginary line that passes through the poles of a planet and on which a planet spins.

cosmos
Another word for the universe.

electromagnetic field
A combination of an electric field and a magnetic field. Light and other types of radiation are a type of moving electromagnetic field.

element
A substance made of atoms that all have the same number of protons.

energy
Energy is what is required for work to be done, such as lifting an object. There are many types of energy, including sound, light, heat, electricity, and mass.

galaxy
A large number of stars, together with planets, gas, dust, and dark matter, that are held together by gravity.

gravity
A force that attracts all objects toward one another. The strength of the force depends on the objects' masses.

greenhouse effect
A process by which certain gases in the atmosphere of a planet trap some of the Sun's heat. As a result, the temperature of the planet rises.

helium
A very light substance that is a gas at all but the lowest temperatures.

hemisphere
Half of a sphere.

hydrogen
A very light substance, the most common in the universe. Most stars are mostly made of hydrogen.

Kuiper Belt object
A lump of ice and other frozen material in orbit beyond Neptune.

lunar
Relating to the Moon.

magnetic field
An area surrounding a moving electric charge or a magnet that produces pushes and pulls on other magnets, charges, and other objects.

mass
A measure of the amount of matter in an object. In a gravitational field, the more mass an object has, the heavier it is.

matter
Substance that has mass and takes up space. Matter exists in four main forms: solid, liquid, gas, and plasma. Particles of antimatter have opposite properties to those of matter. Dark matter is a mysterious substance known to exist only because of the effects of its gravity on ordinary matter.

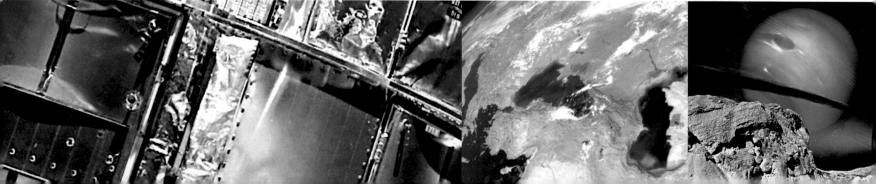

meteor

A meteor is the trail of light in the sky caused by a piece of rock or metal falling from space and burning up in our atmosphere. A meteoroid is the name given to the object before it falls. If part of the object reaches Earth's surface, it is called a meteorite.

moon

A moon is a world that orbits a planet.

nebula

A space object that looks like a cloud. Planetary nebulae are clouds of gas, often round, thrown off by dying stars. They are not connected with planets.

neutrino

A particle, much smaller than an atom, that exists in enormous numbers. They can pass through almost everything—even Earth—without stopping. Neutrinos are almost impossible to detect.

neutron

A neutron is a particle found in the nucleus of every atom except for hydrogen. A neutron star is a dead star in which the gravity is so high that its protons and electrons are crushed together and turn into neutrons.

nuclear

Nuclear means "relating to the nucleus of an atom." Nuclear fusion is the process in which hydrogen is converted into helium in the Sun and most stars, releasing the energy that we see as sunlight and starlight.

nucleus

The core of an atom.

orbit

The path of one object around another in space, such as a planet around a star.

particle

A tiny fragment of matter.

probe

An uncrewed spaceship sent to explore other worlds and gather information.

proton

A particle with a positive electric charge found in the nuclei of all atoms.

radar

A system in which radio waves are beamed toward objects. The way they bounce back tells us about the object. Radar is used to track moving objects, map the surface of planets, and measure their distances from Earth.

radiation

A form of energy that travels through space as electromagnetic waves. Light, radio, infrared, ultraviolet, x-rays, and gamma rays are all types of radiation.

radio

A form of electromagnetic radiation, with waves much longer than light waves.

satellite

An object in orbit around a planet. A moon is a natural satellite; a weather satellite is an artificial one.

solar panel

Solar means "relating to the Sun." A solar panel is a device that converts sunlight into heat or electricity.

star

A glowing mass of gas, held together by gravity.

supernova

A type of exploding star.

volume

A measure of the amount of space that something occupies.

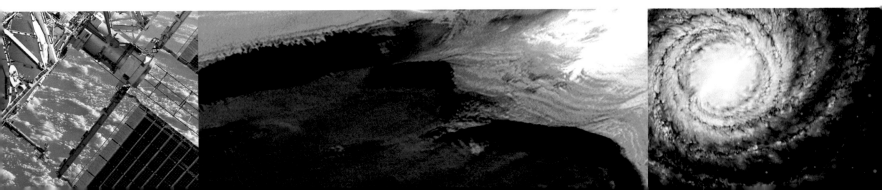

INDEX

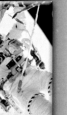

INVESTIGATE

Visit museums to learn about the history of space travel and read books and websites to find out more about stars, the universe, and the planets in our solar system.

time-lapse image of a starry sky

Becoming an astronomer

Anyone can become an astronomer. You don't always need a telescope—stars, planets, satellites, and galaxies can all be seen with the naked eye.

📖 *Kingfisher Pocket Guide to the Night Sky* by Carole Stott (Kingfisher)

✦ Mauna Kea Observatories, 177 Maka'ala Street, Hilo, HI 96720

🌐 **www.ifa.hawaii.edu/mko**

constellation of Orion, the hunter

Constellations

Find out about the myths and legends behind each constellation—a group of stars representing an object, person, animal, or even a monster.

📖 *Stars and Constellations* by Dr. Raman K. Prinja (Heinemann Library)

✦ Rock Creek Planetarium, 5200 Glover Road NW, Washington, DC 20015

🌐 **http://library.thinkquest.org/3645/constellations.html**

a high-tech exhibition at a science museum

Space exploration

Take a trip to a space or science museum to discover how humans and uncrewed probes have traveled through space.

📖 *Kingfisher Voyages: Space* by Dr. Mike Goldsmith (Kingfisher)

 Space Center Houston, 1601 NASA Parkway, Houston, TX 77058

🌐 **www.bbc.co.uk/science/space/universe/exploration/**

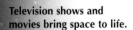
Television shows and movies bring space to life.

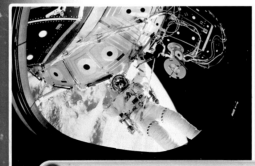

Television and media

Travel into space by watching real movie footage recorded by astronauts or probes. Watch science-fiction movies to spark your imagination about other worlds and alien life!

📖 *A Cinematic History of Sci-Fi and Fantasy* by Mark Wilshin (Raintree)

✦ Stay at home and watch a DVD: *The Planets* (BBC TV)

🌐 **http://dsc.discovery.com/space/**